TOM SAWYER

TOM SAWYER

Mark Twain

Retold by M. W. Thomas

Illustrated by Denis K. Turner

Nelson

THOMAS NELSON AND SONS LTD
Nelson House   Mayfield Road
Walton-on-Thames   Surrey KT12 5PL

51 York Place
Edinburgh EH1 3JD

Yi Xiu Factory Building
Unit 05-06   5th Floor
65 Sims Avenue   Singapore 1438

THOMAS NELSON (HONG KONG) LTD
Toppan Building 10/F
22A Westlands Road   Quarry Bay   Hong Kong

THOMAS NELSON (KENYA) LTD
P.O. Box 18123
Nairobi   Kenya

Distributed in Australia by
Thomas Nelson Australia
480 La Trobe Street
Melbourne   Victoria 3000
and in Sydney, Brisbane, Adelaide and Perth

© *Thomas Nelson and Sons Ltd 1968*

First published by Thomas Nelson and Sons Ltd 1968
Reprinted 1984, 1985
IBSN 0-17-555204-5
NCN 74-ERE-8604-05

Printed in Hong Kong

NOTE

Mark Twain was an American. His real name was Samuel Clemens. He was born in 1835, and many of his books are directly based on his childhood and early life as a printer and journalist, and then as a river pilot on the Mississippi, in the southern part of the United States.

These were the years of the great migration of population southwards and westwards across North America. Countless families were emigrating from Europe, and many of those who had already settled in the eastern states of New England were moving on to find and develop new land and build new towns.

Hannibal, the little town in Missouri where most of Clemen's childhood was spent, had not been founded long when his family first settled there, but it developed fairly rapidly because of its position. As a steamboat port it drew its life from the river, providing a trading centre for many smaller settlements. But apart from the river, life there offered few major excitements. The "frontier", with the thrills of pioneering, had moved farther west. In between steamboat calls Hannibal was a quiet sluggish place, only startled out of the ordinariness of its small town life by an occasional robbery or act of violence. Its people were simple and God-fearing, though much influenced by superstition, as country people often are.

Mark Twain remembered Hannibal chiefly as the background to boyhood adventures. The natural surroundings of the place, the wide prairie in which the farms were set, the woods and cliffs of the river itself, offered the perfect setting for sports and games, exploration and make-believe. He quite certainly used it as a model for the St. Petersburg of *Tom Sawyer* and its sequel *Huckleberry Finn*.

EXERCISES

1. Several passages in *Tom Sawyer* show that St. Petersburg was only a small town. How many of these can you pick out?

2. Tom Sawyer was often in trouble at school. Why was this? If you had to describe Tom's character in six words, what six words would you choose?

3. When he lived by himself Huckleberry Finn was often cold or hungry, but he did not want to live comfortably with the Widow Douglas. Why was this?

4. How many different superstitions can you find mentioned in the story?

One

"Tom!"

No answer.

"Tom!"

No answer.

"Where *is* that boy, I wonder? You Tom!"

The old lady pulled her spectacles down and looked over them; then she put them up and looked out under them. She never looked *through* them for so small a thing as a boy. She seemed puzzled for a moment and said, "Well, if I get hold of you, I'll . . ."

She did not finish, for by this time she was bending down and punching under the bed with the broom—and so she needed breath.

"I never did see the like of that boy!"

She went to the open door and looked down the garden. No Tom. She lifted up her voice and shouted.

"Y-o-u-u *Tom!*"

There was a slight noise behind her, and she turned just in time to catch a small boy by the sleeve of his jacket. "There! I might have thought of that closet. What have you been doing in there?"

"Nothing."

"Nothing! Look at your hands, and look at your mouth. What is it?"

"*I* don't know, aunt."

"Well, *I* know. It's jam, that's what it is. Forty times I've said if you didn't let that jam alone I'd hit you. Hand me that stick."

She swung the stick in the air.

"My! Look behind you, aunt!"

The old lady swung around, and snatched her skirts out of danger. The lad fled as she did so, and jumped over the high fence. His Aunt Polly stood surprised a moment, and then began to laugh.

"Hang the boy! Can't I ever learn anything? Hasn't he played tricks enough like that for me to be looking out for him by this time? I'm not doing my duty by that boy, and that's the truth. Spare the rod and spoil the child, as the good book says. But he's my own dead sister's son, poor thing, and I haven't got the heart to whip him, somehow. He'll stay away from school this afternoon, and I'll just have to make him work on Saturday, when all the other boys are having a holiday. He hates work more than he hates anything else, and I've got to teach him in some way."

Tom *did* stay away from school that afternoon, and he had a very good time. He got back home just in time to help Jim, the small coloured boy, to saw the wood—at least he was there in time to tell Jim what he had been doing, while Jim did nearly all the work. Tom's young half-brother, Sid, had already finished his part of the work (picking up chips), for he was a quiet boy who was no trouble to anyone.

The summer evenings were long. It was not dark yet. Tom was whistling as he strode down the street of the poor little village of St. Petersburg. Soon he stopped whistling. A stranger was before him: a boy a little larger than himself. This boy was well dressed. His cap was a pretty thing. His blue cloth coat was new and smart. He had shoes on, and yet it was only Friday. He even wore a tie, a bright bit of ribbon. Tom stared in surprise. His own clothes seemed very ragged.

Neither boy spoke. If one moved the other moved— they kept face to face and eye to eye all the time. At last Tom said:

"I can lick you!"

"I'd like to see you try it," said the stranger.

"Well, I can do it."

"No, you can't."

"Yes, I can."

"No, you can't."

"Can."

"Can't."

"Get away from here!" cried Tom.

"Get away yourself!" replied the stranger.

Tom made a line in the dust with his big toe, and said:

"I dare you to step over that, and I'll lick you till you can't stand up."

The new boy stepped over at once, and said:

"You said you'd do it, now let's see you."

The next minute both boys were rolling and tumbling in the dirt, tugging at each other's hair and clothes, punching and scratching each other's noses, and covering themselves with dust. Soon Tom was sitting on top of the new boy, hitting him with his fists. The boy tried to free himself. He was crying, mainly because he was angry. At last he gave in, and Tom let him get up, saying, "Now that'll teach you. Better look out who you're fooling with next time."

Tom got home very late that night, and when he climbed quietly through the window, he met his aunt. She saw the dirt on his clothes, and made up her mind that he should work on Saturday instead of having a holiday.

Saturday morning came, and all the world was bright and fresh. There was a song in every heart. Everybody was happy.

Tom appeared on the path with a bucket of white-wash and a long-handled brush. He looked at the fence, and he was filled with sadness. Thirty yards of wide fence nine feet high! He sighed, and dipping his brush in the whitewash, he moved it slowly along the top plank of the fence. He did it again, then sat down on a box.

He began to think of the fun he had planned for this day. Soon the other boys would come tripping along, and they would make fun of him because he had to work. The thought of it burnt him like fire. He emptied his pockets. He had only a few bits of toys and some marbles—not enough to buy even half an hour of freedom. So he gave up the idea of paying the boys to do his work for him. At this dark moment a wonderful thought came to him. He took up his brush again and went quietly to work.

Soon Ben Rogers came along. He was eating an apple. Tom went on whitewashing—took no notice of him. Ben stared a moment, and then said :

"Hi-yi! You're up a stump, ain't you!"

No answer. Tom looked proudly at his work, and then gave his brush another gentle sweep. Ben came close up to him. Tom's mouth watered for the apple, but he stuck to his work. Ben said:

"Hello, old chap! You got to work, hey?"

"Why, it's you, Ben! I didn't notice you."

"Say, I'm going swimming," replied Ben. "Don't you wish you could come with me? But of course you'd rather work, wouldn't you? 'Course you would!"

Tom looked at him and said:

"What do you call work?"

"Why, ain't that work?"

Tom went on whitewashing, and said carelessly:

"Well, perhaps it is, and perhaps it ain't. All I know is, it suits me."

"Oh, come now," said Ben, "you don't mean to say you like it?"

The brush went on moving.

"Like it?" said Tom at last. "Well, why shouldn't I like it? Does a boy get a chance to whitewash a fence every day?"

Ben stopped eating his apple. Tom swept his brush back and forth—stepped back to look at his work—added a touch here and there. Ben watched every move. He was getting more and more interested. At last he said:

"Say, Tom, let me whitewash a little."

Tom thought for a minute. He was going to hand over his brush, but he changed his mind. "No, no," he said. "It wouldn't do, Ben. You see, Aunty Polly is very particular about this fence. It's got to be done very carefully. I reckon there ain't one boy in a hundred, perhaps two hundred, that can do it the way it's got to be done."

"Is that so?" said Ben. "Oh, come now, just let me try—only a little. I'd let you, if you were me, Tom."

"Ben, I'd like to. But Aunt Polly—well, Jim wanted to do it, but she wouldn't let him. Sid wanted to do it, but she wouldn't let Sid. Now, don't you see how I am fixed? If you were to do this fence, and anything happened to it . . ."

"Oh, shucks; I'll be just as careful as you. Now, let me try. Say—I'll give you a bit of my apple!"

"Well, here," said Tom. He began to hand over the brush, but changed his mind. "No, Ben," he continued, "I daren't. . . ."

"I'll give you all the apple!" cried Ben.

Tom gave up the brush. And while Ben Rogers worked and sweated in the sun, he sat on a barrel in the shade close by, swung his legs, ate his apple, and made plans for the next boys who came along.

There were many of them. They came to make fun of Tom, but they stayed to whitewash. By the time Ben was fagged out, Tom had sold the next chance to Billy Fisher for a new kite. When Billy had had enough, Johnny Miller bought *his* chance for a dead rat and a string to swing it with. So it went on, hour after hour.

When the middle of the afternoon came, Tom was quite rich. Besides the things I have mentioned, he had twelve marbles, a piece of blue glass to look through, a key that wouldn't open anything, a piece of chalk, a tin soldier, two tadpoles, a kitten with only one eye, an iron door-knob, a dog collar—but no dog—the handle of a knife, and four pieces of orange peel. He had had a nice, good, easy time all the while, plenty of company —and the fence had three coats of whitewash on it. If

he hadn't run out of whitewash, he would have ruined every boy in the village.

Tom now went skipping along past the house where Jeff Thatcher lived. In the garden he saw a new girl— a lovely blue-eyed girl with yellow hair in two long pig-tails. He looked hard at this new angel till he knew that she had seen him. Then he pretended he did not know she was there, and began to "show off" in all sorts of ways in order to make her think well of him. She stopped a moment on the steps of her house, and then moved to the door.

Tom sighed, but his face lit up at once because she threw a pansy over the fence just as she went in. The boy picked up the flower, and put it inside his jacket, next to his heart.

Two

Monday morning came. Tom was always unhappy on Monday morning, because it began another week of school. He was making his way slowly towards the school when he met Huckleberry Finn, a young rascal who was hated by all the mothers because he was lazy and bad—and because all their children liked him so. Tom, like all the other boys, had been given orders not to play with him. So he played with him every time he got a chance.

Huckleberry was always dressed in old clothes big enough for a man. His hat was a vast ruin; his coat, when he wore one, hung nearly to his heels. He came and went as he pleased. He slept on door-steps in fine weather, and in empty barrels when it was wet. He never went to school or to church. He could go fishing or swimming when he liked, and he could sit up as late as he wished. He never had to wash, nor put on clean clothes. Tom called out to this young man, and said:

"Hello, Huckleberry!"

"Hello yourself."

"What's that you've got?"

"Dead cat," replied Huckleberry.

"Let me see him, Huck. My, he's pretty stiff. Where did you get him?"

"Bought him from a boy."

"Say—what is dead cats good for, Huck?"

"Good for? To cure warts[1] with."

"How do you cure them with dead cats?"

"Why, you take your cat and go in the graveyard about midnight, where some wicked person has been buried. When it's midnight, a devil will come for the body. Sometimes two or three will come. You can't see them, you can only hear something like the wind, or you may hear them talk. When they are taking the body away, you throw your cat after them, and say, 'Devil follow the corpse,[2] cat follow devil, warts follow cat, I've finished with you!' That will move any wart."

"Sounds right," said Tom. "Did you ever try it, Huck?"

"No, but old Mother Hopkins told me."

"Well, it must be true then, because they say she's a witch. When are you going to try the cat?"

"To-night. I expect the devils will come for old Hoss Williams to-night."

"But they buried him on Saturday, Huck. Didn't the devils get him Saturday night?"

"Why, how you talk! How could their magic work till midnight? And then it's Sunday. Devils don't slosh around much on Sunday, I reckon."

"I never thought of that," said Tom. "That's true. Can I go with you?"

"Of course—if you're not afraid."

"Afraid? That's not likely. Will you miaow like a cat when you call for me?"

[1] Wart—a little lump on the skin   [2] corpse—a dead body

"Yes, and you miaow back if you get the chance."

"All right. I will. Goodbye!"

When Tom reached the little school, he strode in quickly, as if he had come along at a great speed. He hung his hat on a peg, and sat down at his desk. The master was half asleep in his great arm-chair. He looked up when Tom came in.

"Thomas Sawyer!"

Tom knew that when his name was called in full, it meant trouble.

"Sir!"

"Come up here. Now, sir, why are you late again?"

Tom was going to tell a lie, but he saw two long tails of yellow hair hanging down a back that he knew. It was the girl he had seen in the garden, and *the only empty desk* on the girls' side of the class was next to hers. He said:

"I STOPPED TO TALK TO HUCKLEBERRY FINN!"

The master just looked at him. The hum of study stopped; the pupils wondered if this silly boy had gone mad. The master said:

"You—you did what?"

"Stopped to talk to Huckleberry Finn."

"Thomas Sawyer," said the master, "this is the most amazing thing I have ever heard. Take off your jacket."

The master beat him till his arm was tired. Then came the order:

"Now, go and sit with the girls! And let this be a lesson to you."

Tom had been hoping that this would be part of his punishment. He went to the empty desk, next to the girl with the yellow hair, and sat down. Soon he began to look at her. She turned her head away for a minute, and moved away from him. When she looked round again, a peach was lying there in front of her. She pushed it away. Tom gently put it back. She pushed it away again. Then Tom wrote on his slate, "Please take it—I've got more."

The girl looked at the words, but made no sign. Now the boy began to draw something on his slate, hiding his work with his left hand. For a time the girl took no notice, but at last she whispered:

"Let me see it."

Tom moved his hand, and showed her a drawing of a house, with smoke coming from the chimney. The girl looked at it for a moment, and then she said:

"It's ever so nice. I wish I could draw."

"It's easy," whispered Tom, "I'll teach you."

"Oh, will you? When?"

"At noon. Do you go home to dinner?"

"I'll stay if you will."

"Good—that's a go. What's your name?"

"Becky Thatcher. What's yours? Oh, I know. It's Thomas Sawyer."

"That's what they call me when they whip me. I'm Tom when I'm good. You call me Tom, will you?"

"Yes."

Now Tom began to write something on the slate, hiding the words from the girl. She begged him to let her see. Tom said:

"Oh, it ain't anything."

"Yes, it is."

"No, it ain't. You don't want to see. You'll tell."

"No, I won't—indeed I won't," replied Becky.

She put her small hand on his, and there was a little fight. At last Tom let his hand slip, and the girl could see the words: "*I love you.*"

"Oh, you bad thing," said Becky; and she hit his hand. But her face grew red, and she looked pleased.

When school broke up at noon, Tom flew to Becky Thatcher, and whispered in her ear:

"Put on your bonnet, and pretend you're going home. When you get to the corner, give the rest of the girls the slip, turn down the lane, and come back. I'll go round the other way and meet you."

In a little while the two met at the bottom of the lane, and when they got back to school they had it all to themselves. They sat together, with a slate before them, and Tom gave Becky the pencil. He held her hand in his, moving it so that soon they had drawn another house. Then they started talking.

"Do you love rats?" said Tom.

"No, I hate them."

"Well, I do too—live ones. But I mean dead ones, to swing around your head with a string."

"No, I don't care for rats, anyway. What *I* like is chewing-gum," said Becky.

"Do you? I've got some. I'll let you chew it a bit, but you must give it back to me."

So they chewed it in turn, and swung their legs happily against the bench.

"Say, Becky," said Tom at last, "were you ever engaged?"

"What's that?"

"Why, engaged to be married."

"No."

"Would you like to?"

"I don't know. What's it like?" said Becky.

"Like? Well, it ain't like anything. You only just tell a boy that you won't ever have anybody but him, ever, ever, *ever*, and then you kiss, and that's all. Anybody can do it."

Tom passed his arm about her waist, and whispered ever so softly, with his mouth close to her ear. And then he said:

"Now you whisper it to me—just the same."

She bent round till her breath stirred his hair, then she whispered, "I—love—you. I'll never love anybody but you, Tom, and I'll never marry anybody but you, and you ain't ever to marry anybody but me, either."

"Of course," said Tom. "That's *part* of it. And always, coming to school, or when we're going home, you must walk with me—and you choose me and I choose you at parties, because that's the way you do when you're engaged."

"It's so nice. I never heard of it before."

"Oh, it's ever so jolly. Why me and Amy Lawrence . . ."

The big eyes told Tom the mistake he had made, and he stopped.

"Oh, Tom! Then I ain't the first you've been engaged to!"

Becky began to cry. Tom said:

"Oh, don't cry, Becky. I don't love her any more."

"Yes, you do, Tom—you know you do."

Tom tried to put his arm about her neck, but she pushed him away and turned her face to the wall, and went on crying. Tom tried again, with gentle words, but again she pushed him away. Then his pride was up. He walked away and went outside. He stood about, restless and unhappy, for a while, glancing at the door every now and then, hoping she would feel sorry and come to find him. But she did not. Then he began to feel badly, and fear that he was in the wrong. He went back into the room.

She was still standing in the corner, crying with her face to the wall. Tom did not know what to do, but he said :

"Becky, I—I don't love anybody but you."

No reply.

"Becky, won't you say something ?"

She did not answer.

Tom got out his greatest treasure, an iron knob, and pushed it in front of her so that she could see it, and said :

"Please, Becky, won't you take it ?"

She struck it to the floor. Then Tom marched out of the school-room and over the hills and far away.

Soon Becky began to change her mind. She ran to the door; he was not in sight; she flew round the playground; he was not there. Then she called :

"Tom! Come back, Tom!"

She listened, but there was no answer. So she sat down to cry again.

Tom did not come back to school that day.

Three

At half-past nine that night, Tom and Sid were sent to bed as usual. Sid was soon asleep, but Tom lay waiting for Huck's signal. The clock had struck ten, when he heard a "miaow" from the garden, and a minute later he was dressed and out of the window. He "miaow'd" once or twice as he went, and soon he came upon Huckleberry Finn with his dead cat. The two boys moved off through the darkness, and at the end of half an hour they came to the graveyard.

The graveyard was on a hill, about a mile and a half from the village. Grass and weeds grew everywhere. A wind was blowing through the trees, and Tom feared it might be the spirits of the dead. They found the grave they were looking for, and lay down under three tall trees. They waited without a word for a long time. The hooting of an owl was all they could hear. At last Tom whispered:

"Huck, do you think the dead people like us to be here?"

"I wish I knew," replied Huckleberry. "It's awful lonely, ain't it?"

There was a pause, then Tom said:

"Say, Hucky, do you think Hoss Williams can hear us talking?"

"Of course he can. At least his spirit can hear us."

"I wish I'd said *Mister* Williams," said Tom. "But I didn't think. Everybody calls him Hoss."

They were quiet for a time, and then Tom took his friend's arm, and said:

"*Sh!*"

"What is it, Tom?"

"*Sh!* There it is again. Didn't you hear it?"

"Lord, Tom, they're coming. What shall we do?"

"I don't know. They can see in the dark like cats. I wish I hadn't come. Listen!"

The low sound of voices came from the far end of the graveyard. Some men were walking towards them, swinging a lantern.

"They are *humans*," said Huck. "One of them is old Muff Potter. I know his voice."

"All right; keep still. Say, Huck, I know another of those voices. It's Injun Joe, the half-breed.[1] What can they be doing?"

The three men had now reached the grave. They were standing a few feet from the boys' hiding-place.

"Here it is," said a third voice. The speaker held up the lantern as he spoke, and the boys saw that it was young Dr. Robinson.

Potter and Injun Joe were carrying a rope and two shovels. They began to open the grave.[2]

"Hurry, men!" said the doctor in a low voice. "The moon might come out at any minute."

[1] half-breed—a man who is half white and half Indian
[2] At this time it was often impossible for doctors to get the corpses they needed in order to learn more about the human body. Sometimes they paid men to dig up bodies that had just been buried

The two men went on digging. At last a shovel struck upon the coffin, and in a minute or two they had got it out on the ground. They knocked off the lid, and Potter took out a large knife and cut off a piece of rope to tie up the body of the dead man.

"Now it's ready, doctor," he said, "and you'll just pay another five pounds, or here it stays."

"That's the talk!" said Injun Joe.

"Look here; what does this mean?" said Dr. Robinson. "I've paid you already."

"Yes, and you have done more than that," said Injun Joe. "Five years ago you drove me away from your father's kitchen one night when I came to ask for something to eat. You said I was not there for any good; and when I swore that I would get even with you, your father had me put in prison. Did you think I'd forget? And now I've got you!"

He held his fist in the doctor's face. The doctor hit out at him, and knocked him to the ground. Potter dropped his knife, and cried:

"Here, now, don't you hit my friend!"

The next minute he threw himself on the doctor, and the two of them were fighting. All at once, the doctor got free and, snatching up a heavy board from the head of the grave, he knocked Potter to the ground. At the same instant, Injun Joe saw his chance. Snatching up Potter's knife, he drove it into the doctor's breast. The young man fell upon Potter, covering him with his blood. It was a terrible sight, and the two frightened boys went speeding away in the dark.

Presently, when the moon came out, Injun Joe was standing over the two fallen men. The doctor gave a long sigh, and lay still. Injun Joe robbed his body, and then put the deadly knife in Potter's open right hand. Three—four—five minutes passed, and then Potter began to stir. His hand closed upon the knife. He lifted it up, looked quickly at it, and let it fall. His eyes met Joe's.

"Lord, what's this, Joe?" he said. "What did you do it for?"

"I! I didn't do it."

Potter grew white.

"I should not have been drinking to-night," he said. "I'm all in a muddle. Tell me, Joe—*honest* now—did I do it? I never meant to. Tell me how it was, Joe. Oh, it's awful—and him so young."

"Why, you two were fighting, and he hit you with

the board. You fell flat; then up you came, snatched the knife, and stuck it into him just as he hit you again. And here you've been lying dead as a door-nail till now."

"Oh, I didn't know what I was doing. It must have been the drink. I never used a knife before. Joe, don't tell anybody! Say you won't tell, Joe. I always liked you and stood up for you. You won't tell, will you, Joe?" And the poor fellow dropped on his knees before the murderer.

"No, you have always been fair with me, Muff Potter, and I won't tell anybody. There, now, that's all I can say."

"Oh, Joe, you're an angel. I'll thank you for this as long as I live." And Potter began to cry.

"Come, now," said Injun Joe, "that's enough of that. You be off that way, and I'll go this way. Move, now, and don't leave any tracks behind you."

Potter started off at a run. The half-breed stood looking after him. He said to himself:

"If he's as muddled as he looks, he won't think about the knife till he's gone so far that he'll be afraid to come back for it. How silly he is!"

Two or three minutes later, the murdered man, the corpse, the lidless coffin, and the open grave were alone under the moon. Everything was quiet again.

Four

The two boys ran on and on towards the village. They looked back over their shoulders from time to time, as if they were afraid they might be followed.

"I only hope we can get to the old leather-factory before we break down!" whispered Tom. "I can't stand this much longer."

Huckleberry was breathing hard, and did not reply. At last they burst through the open door.

"Huckleberry," said Tom, "what do you think will come of this?"

"If Dr. Robinson dies, somebody will be hanged."

Tom thought awhile, and then he said:

"Who will tell? We?"

"What are you talking about? If something happened, and they didn't hang Injun Joe, why he'd kill us some time or other just as sure as we're lying here."

"That's just what I was thinking, Huck."

"If anybody tells, let Muff Potter do it, if he's silly enough. He's nearly always drunk, anyway."

Tom said nothing. He went on thinking. At last he said:

"Huck, Muff Potter knows nothing about it. How can he tell?"

"Why doesn't he know anything?"

"Because he'd just been knocked out when Injun Joe killed the doctor. Do you think he could see anything? Do you think he knew anything?"

"By hokey, that's so, Tom."

After another silence, Tom said:

"Hucky, are you sure you can keep quiet?"

"Tom, we *must* keep quiet. You know that. Injun Joe would kill us if we said anything and they didn't hang him. Now look here, Tom, let's swear to one another—that's what we've got to do—swear to say nothing to anybody."

"I agree, Huck. It's the best thing. Would you just hold hands and swear that we . . ."

"Oh, no, that wouldn't do for this. That's good enough for little ordinary things—but there ought to be writing about a big thing like this. And blood."

Tom picked up a clean white board that lay in the moonlight, took a little piece of chalk from his pocket, and wrote out these lines:

Huck Finn and Tom Sawyer swears they will keep quiet about this and they wish they may Drop down dead in their tracks if they ever tell and Rot.

Each boy pricked his thumb and squeezed out a drop of blood. At last, after many squeezes, Tom managed to sign his initials, using his little finger for a pen. Then he showed Huckleberry how to make an H and an F; it was finished. They buried the board close to the wall.

When Tom crept in at his bedroom window, the night was almost gone. He undressed, and fell asleep, thinking that nobody knew that he had left the house. He did not know that the gently snoring Sid was awake, and had been so for an hour.

When Tom woke up, Sid was dressed and gone. It was quite light. He was surprised. Why had he not been called as usual? In five minutes he was dressed and downstairs. The family had finished breakfast. Nobody said anything to him. They turned their eyes away, and he sat down in silence.

After breakfast his aunt took him aside. She cried over him, and asked him how he could go and break her old heart like this. It was worse than a hundred whippings, and Tom's heart was very touched. He cried and asked his aunt to pardon him, and she told him to get ready for school.

He went along the road, feeling very sad. When he got to school, he went to his seat, put his elbows on the desk, and looked at the wall. His elbow was against something hard. He picked it up with a sigh. It was in a paper. He opened it. Another long sigh followed, and his heart broke. It was his knob!

It was about noon that the whole village heard the terrible news of the murder. The news flew from man to man, from group to group, from house to house. Of course, the schoolmaster gave a holiday that afternoon. A knife, covered with blood, had been found close to the murdered man, and somebody said it belonged to Muff Potter. They had searched the town for him, but he could not be found. Horsemen had been sent down all the roads, and the sheriff was sure he would be caught before night.

The people were making their way towards the graveyard. Tom joined them, and when he came to the spot, he felt somebody at his arm. He turned, and saw Huckleberry Finn.

"Poor fellow!" "Poor young fellow!" "This ought to be a lesson to the grave-robbers!" "They will hang Muff Potter for this if they catch him!" This is what people were saying.

Tom began to shake from head to foot, for his eye fell upon the face of Injun Joe. Now the crowd began to move about, and voices shouted, "It's him! it's him! he's coming himself!"

"Who? Who?" from twenty voices.

"Muff Potter!"

"Hello, he's stopped! Look out, he's turning! Don't let him get away!"

"What cheek!" said one of the crowd. "He wanted to come and take a quiet look at what he had done—didn't expect to see anyone."

The crowd parted now, and the sheriff came through, leading Potter by the arm. The poor fellow's face was white, and his eyes showed how frightened he was. When he stood before the murdered man, he shook like a leaf, and he put his face in his hands and burst into tears.

"I didn't do it, friends," he cried; "upon my word I didn't do it!"

"Who said you did?" shouted a voice.

At this, Potter lifted his face and looked around him sadly. He saw Injun Joe, and said:

"Oh, Injun Joe, you promised me you'd never . . ."

"Is that your knife?" The knife was pushed in front of him by the sheriff.

Potter would have fallen if they had not caught him. Then he said:

"Something told me that if I didn't come back and

get . . ." He waved his hands and said, "Tell them, Joe, tell them—it's no use any more."

Then Huckleberry and Tom stood silently staring and heard the half-breed liar tell his story. They thought he would be struck dead for his wickedness. But when he had finished, and still stood alive and whole, they decided that he must have sold himself to the devil. They made up their minds to watch him, hoping that they might see his terrible master.

For a week after this Tom got little sleep because of his awful secret. At breakfast one morning, Sid said:

"Tom, you move around and talk so much in your sleep that you keep me awake half the time."

Tom grew white and dropped his eyes.

"It's a bad sign," said Aunt Polly. "What have you got on your mind, Tom?"

"Nothing. Nothing that I know of." But the boy's hand shook so much that he spilled his coffee.

"And you do talk such stuff," Sid said. "Last night you said, 'It's blood, it's blood, that's what it is!' You said that time after time. And you said, 'Leave me alone. I'm going to tell.' Tell what? What is it you'll tell?"

"Ah, it's that terrible murder," said Aunt Polly. "I dream about it nearly every night myself. Sometimes I dream that I did it myself."

Sid seemed to think this might be so. After that, Tom pretended that his tooth ached, and he tied up his jaws every night so that he could not talk in his sleep any more. He never knew that Sid often slipped the bandage off, listened to what he said, and then put the bandage back in its place.

Every day or two, Tom went to the window of the little prison where Muff Potter was kept, and pushed small parcels through to the "murderer". The prison was a little brick hut that stood at the edge of the village. There were no guards, since it did not often hold a prisoner. The men of the village wanted to punish Injun Joe for body-snatching, but he was such a dangerous man that nobody was willing to take the lead.

Five

Tom was very sad and lonely. Nobody loved him. He made up his mind to run away from home and be a pirate. He was walking along when he met his friend Joe Harper. Joe's mother had whipped him for drinking some cream, and he, too, was going to run away.

The two boys set out to find Huckleberry Finn. They told him what they were going to do, and he said he would go with them to Jackson's Island. This was a long island three miles below St. Petersburg, at a point where the river was just over a mile wide. It was a good place for pirates because nobody lived there. They would meet at midnight at a lonely place on the bank of the river. Each of them would steal some food, and then they would take a boat, and cross the river to the island.

About midnight Tom came to the meeting-place carrying a boiled ham. The stars were shining, and it was very quiet and still. He stopped near some thick bushes, and gave a low whistle. A voice said:

"Who goes there?"

"Tom Sawyer, the Black Pirate. Name your names."

"Huck Finn the Red-handed, and Joe Harper, the Terror of the Seas."

"Good. Give the sign."

Two low voices said the same awful word:

"BLOOD!"

Then Tom picked up his ham, and went to join his friends. The Terror of the Seas had brought a side of bacon, and Finn the Red-handed had stolen some tobacco and pipes. They found a boat, and soon they were in the middle of the river on their way to Jackson's Island.

At two o'clock in the morning they landed on the shore. A fire was lit, and soon they were cooking some bacon for their supper. When they had eaten all they could, they lay down on the grass and smoked their pipes.

"Ain't it jolly?" said Joe.

"It's *fine*," said Tom,

"What would the boys say if they could see us?"

"Say? Well, they'd just die to be here—hey, Hucky?"

"I reckon so," said Huckleberry; "*I* don't want anything better than this. I don't ever get enough to eat—and nobody can come and kick me here."

"It's just the life for me," said Tom. "You don't have to get up in the morning, and you don't have to wash and go to school. A pirate doesn't have to do *anything*."

"What *do* pirates have to do?" asked Huck.

Tom said:

"Oh, they just have a good time—take ships, and burn them, and get the money and bury it in their island where there are ghosts to watch it, and kill everybody in the ships."

"And they carry the women to the island," said Joe; "but they don't kill the women."

"No," said Tom, "they don't kill the women—they're too beautiful."

"And they wear the finest clothes," said Joe. "All gold and silver and diamonds."

"Who?" said Huck.

"Why, the pirates."

Huck looked sadly at his own clothes.

"I reckon I'm not dressed like a pirate," he said. "I've got no clothes but these."

But the other boys told him the fine clothes would come fast enough, and his poor rags would do to begin with.

Soon they stopped talking. The pipe fell from Tom's hand, and the three pirates dropped off to sleep.

When Tom woke up in the morning, he wondered where he was. He sat up and rubbed his eyes and looked around; then he remembered. He woke up the other pirates, and in a minute or two they were tumbling over each other in the river. They came out feeling very happy, and soon they had their fire burning again. While Joe was cutting some bacon for breakfast, Tom and Huck caught some fish. They cooked them with the bacon, and had a fine meal.

They lay around in the shade after breakfast, and then went off through the woods. They had a swim about every hour, and it was the middle of the afternoon when they got back to their camp. They ate some of Tom's ham, and then sat down under the trees to talk. Suddenly they heard a loud bang from down the river.

"What is that?" said Joe, under his breath.

"I wonder?" said Tom in a low voice.

"It isn't thunder," said Huckleberry, "because thunder . . ."

"Hush!" said Tom; "listen—don't talk."

They waited a long time, and then they heard the same noise again.

"Let's go and see."

The boys jumped to their feet, and ran to the edge of the river. Through the bushes they could see that the little ferry-boat was coming slowly down the river.

She was crowded with people, but the boys could not see what they were doing. Soon a great puff of white smoke burst from the side of the boat, and the same bang was heard again.

"I know now!" cried Tom. "Somebody is drowned!"

"That's it," said Huck. "They did that last summer when Bill Turner got drowned. They shoot a cannon over the water, and that makes the body come up to the top."

"By jings, I wish I was over there now," said Joe.

"I do too," said Huck. "I'd give a lot to know who it is."

The boys listened and went on watching. At last a sudden thought struck Tom, and he said:

"Boys, I know who is drowned: it's us!"

This was fine. Their friends were missing them. Hearts were breaking for them. People were crying because they had been so unkind to the poor boys. It was good to be a pirate, after all.

As night came on, the ferry-boat went back up the river, and the pirates made their way once more to the camp. They were feeling very happy now. They caught fish, cooked supper and ate it, and then they began to wonder what the people of the village were thinking and saying about them. At last they stopped talking, and sat looking quietly into the fire. Tom and Joe were soon thinking that their friends at home were not enjoying this as much as they were.

The stars came out, and Huck began to feel sleepy. Soon he was snoring. Joe followed next. Tom lay upon his elbow for some time, watching the other two. At last he got up quietly and went into the long grass. He picked up two pieces of thin white wood and, kneeling down by the fire, he wrote something upon each of them with a piece of red chalk. One he put in his jacket pocket, and the other he put in Joe's hat. He also put into the hat some of his treasures—a rubber ball, three fish-hooks and a few marbles. Then he crept softly into the trees and began to run towards the river.

A few minutes later he was swimming through the dark water to the bank on the other side. At last he got there and pulling himself out, he found that he was near the village. Racing through the lonely lanes, it was not long before he reached his aunt's back fence. He climbed over, and looked in at the sitting-room window, for a light was burning there. There sat Aunt Polly, Sid, his cousin Mary, and Joe Harper's mother, all together, talking.

They were by the bed, and the bed was between them and the door. Tom went to the door, turned the handle very gently, pushed it open, and squeezed through on his knees.

"What makes the candle blow like that?" said Aunt Polly. Tom hurried up. "Why, that door's open, I think. Go along and shut it, Sid."

Tom got under the bed just in time. He lay there for a bit, and then crept to where he could almost touch his aunt's foot.

"But as I was saying," said Aunt Polly, "he wasn't really bad. He never did any harm. Sometimes he was rather wild, but he was the best boy that ever was," and she began to cry.

"It was the same with my Joe," said Mrs. Harper. "He was as kind as he could be—and bless me, to think I went and whipped him for taking that cream, when all the time I had thrown it out myself because it had gone bad. And I shall never see him again in this world, never, never, never, poor boy!" And Mrs. Harper burst into tears.

"I hope Tom's better off where he is," said Sid; "but if he'd been better in some ways . . ."

"*Sid!*" said Aunt Polly. "Not a word against my Tom, now that he's gone! God will take care of him.

Oh, Mrs. Harper, I don't know how to give him up. He was such a good boy to me!"

By this time, Tom was crying quietly to himself, but he went on listening. He heard them say that this was Wednesday night. If the boys were still missing on Saturday prayers would be said for them in the church.

Soon Mrs. Harper said good-night, and turned to go. Sid and Mary went off still crying, and Aunt Polly knelt down and prayed for Tom before she got into bed.

At last she fell asleep. Tom stood up and looked down at her, feeling very sorry for what he had done. Then he took the piece of wood from his pocket, and was going to place it by the candle when a thought came to him. He put the wood back into his pocket, bent over and kissed his aunt, and then quietly left the room, closing the door behind him.

It was day-light when he got back to the island. As he crept up to the camp, he heard Joe say:

"Tom will come back, Huck. He won't leave us. No pirate would run away, and Tom's too good for that sort of thing. I wonder what he's doing?"

"Well, these things are ours, aren't they?"

"Not yet Huck. The writing says they are if he ain't back to breakfast."

"Which he is!" said Tom, stepping into the camp.

They had a fine breakfast of bacon and fish, and while they were eating it Tom told them what he had been doing. Then he lay down in the shade to get some sleep, while the other pirates went off to fish.

Six

The gang had a fine time during the next two days. They went swimming in the river, and sometimes they got out their marbles and played with them. But by Friday morning they were not quite so happy. They began to look across the wide river to the village on the other side. Tom found himself writing " *Becky* " in the sand with his big toe. Joe was feeling very sad, because he wanted to go home. Huck was beginning to be sorry for himself, too. Tom did not know what to do. He had a secret, but he was not ready to tell it yet.

"Oh, boys," said Joe at last, poking the sand with a stick, "let's give it up. I want to go home. It's so lonely here."

"Oh, no, Joe," said Tom, "you'll soon feel better. Just think of the fishing we can have here."

"I don't want to fish. I want to go home."

"But, Joe, there ain't another swimming-place like this anywhere."

"Swimming's no good. I don't like it much when there's nobody to tell me not to go in. I'm going home."

"Oh, shucks! You want to see your mother, I reckon."

"Yes, I *do* want to see my mother, and you would too, if you had one."

"Well, we'll let the cry-baby go home to his mother, won't we, Huck? Poor thing—does it want to see its mother? And so it shall. *You* like it here, don't you, Huck? We'll stay, won't we?"

Huck said, "Y-e-s—" but he didn't really mean it.

"I'll never speak to you again as long as I live," said Joe. And he began to move away.

"Who cares?" said Tom. "Go home, if you want to. Oh, you're a nice pirate. Huck and me ain't cry-babies. We'll stay, won't we, Huck? Let him go if he wants to. I reckon we can get along without him."

Joe began to move towards the river. Tom's heart sank, and he looked at Huck. Huck could not bear the look, and dropped his eyes. Then he said:

"I want to go, too, Tom. It was getting very lonely, and now it'll be worse. Let's go too, Tom."

"I won't. You can both go if you want to. I'm going to stay."

"Tom, I want to go."

"Well, go. Who's stopping you?"

"Tom," said Huck, "I wish you'd come with us. Now you think about it. We'll wait for you when we get to the other side."

"Well, you'll wait a long time, that's all."

Huck started sadly away. Tom stood looking after him. He hoped the boys would stop, but they still went slowly on. Then he ran after them, shouting:

"Wait! wait! I want to tell you something."

They stopped and turned round. When he got to where they were he began to tell them his secret. When he had done, they clapped their hands and said it was fine. Then Huck brought out his pipes and tobacco, and they stretched themselves out on the ground and had a quiet smoke.

All the people in the little town of St. Petersburg were very sad the next afternoon. The Harpers and Aunt Polly's family were dressed in black. Everything was quiet and still. Prayers had been said that morning for the missing boys, and there was to be a service in the church on Sunday morning.

When Sunday came the bells began to ring, and the villagers made their way slowly to the church. It had never been so full before. Aunt Polly came in, followed by Sid and Mary, and then by the Harper family, all in deep black. When they had taken their seats in the front row, the minister stood up and said a prayer. A hymn was then sung and after that the minister started to speak about the poor dead boys. He said how sweet and good they were, and how much they were missed. He went on till all the people were crying. He was crying himself before he had finished.

There was a little noise at the back of the church, but nobody noticed it. A minute later, the door was softly opened, and the minister looked up and stood amazed! First one and then another pair of eyes followed the minister's, and then everybody rose and started while the three dead boys came marching in, Tom in the lead, Joe next, and Huck, in his long rags, behind.

Aunt Polly, Mary, and the Harpers threw their arms around the missing boys, and covered them with kisses. Then the minister shouted at the top of his voice:

" 'Praise God, from whom all blessings flow'— SING—and put your hearts into it!"

And they did.

That was Tom's great secret—to come back home with the other pirates and listen to the service that was to be held for them. They had paddled over the river on a log, at dusk on Saturday; they had slept in the woods at the edge of the town till nearly day-light; and had then crept through back lanes and finished their sleep among the benches at the back of the church.

At breakfast, on Monday morning, Aunt Polly and Mary were very loving to Tom. As they were talking, Aunt Polly said :

"Well, I don't say it wasn't a fine joke, Tom, to make us all unhappy while you boys were having a good time, but if you could come over on a log, you could have come over and told me you weren't dead."

"Yes, you could have done that, Tom," said Mary; "and I think you would if you had thought of it."

"Would you, Tom?" said Aunt Polly. "Say, now, would you, if you had thought of it?"

"I—well, I don't know. It would have spoiled everything."

"Tom, I hope you loved me at least that much," said Aunt Polly.

"Now, Auntie, you know I do love you," said Tom. "I wish now I'd thought, but I dreamed about you, anyway. That's something, ain't it?"

"It ain't much—a cat does that much—but it's better than nothing. What did you dream?"

"Why, Wednesday night I dreamt that you were sitting over there by the bed, and Sid was sitting by the wood-box, and Mary next to him."

"Well, so we did."

"And I dreamt that Joe Harper's mother was here."

"Why, she *was* here! Did you dream any more?"

"Oh, lots. But I can't remember now."

"Well, try, can't you?"

"Somehow it seemed to me that the wind—the wind blowed the—the . . ."

"Try harder, Tom! The wind did blow something, come!"

Tom pressed his fingers to his head for a minute, and then said:

"I've got it now! I've got it now! It blowed the candle!"

"Mercy on us! Go on, Tom, go on!"

"And I think you said, 'Why, that door . . .'"

"Go on, Tom!"

"Just let me think a minute—just a minute. Oh, yes, you said the door must be open."

"As I'm sitting here, so I did!" cried Aunt Polly. "Didn't I, Mary? Go on!"

"And then—and then—well, I'm not sure, but it seems as if you made Sid go and—and . . ."

"Well? Well? What did I make him do, Tom? What did I make him do?"

"You made him—you—Oh, you made him shut it!"

"Well, I never heard anything like that in all my life. Go on, Tom!"

"Oh, it's all getting as clear as day now. Next you said I wasn't bad, only a bit wild."

"And so it was! Well. Go on!"

"And then you began to cry."

"So I did. So I did. Not the first time, neither. And then . . ."

"Then Mrs. Harper began to cry, and said Joe was just the same, and she wished she hadn't whipped him for taking the cream when she'd thrown it out herself . . ."

"Tom, this is wonderful. Go on!"

"And then Sid he said—he said . . ."

"I don't think I said anything," said Sid.

"Yes, you did, Sid," said Mary.

"Shut up, and let Tom go on," said Aunt Polly. "What did Sid say, Tom?"

"He said—I think he said he hoped I was better off where I was gone to, but if I'd been better sometimes . . ."

"There, do you hear that? It was his very words!"

"And you shut him up sharp."

"I know I did. There must have been an angel there.

Tom you couldn't have told it better if you'd seen it. Go on."

"And then there was some talk about saying prayers for us, and then you and Mrs. Harper cried, and she went."

"It happened just so. And then what?"

"Then I thought you prayed for me. And you went to bed, and I was so sorry that I wrote on a piece of wood, ' We ain't dead—we are only off being pirates,' and put it on the table by the candle. And then you looked so good, lying there asleep, that I thought I went and bent over and kissed you."

"Did you, Tom, did you? I forgive you just everything for that. Here's a big apple I've been saving for you, if you were ever found again—now go along to school. I'm so glad I've got you back. Go along, Sid and Mary—take yourselves off."

The children left for school, and the old lady went to call on Mrs. Harper to tell her about Tom's wonderful dream.

Seven

Tom made up his mind that he would have no more to do with Becky Thatcher. The next time he saw her in the school playground, he moved away and joined a group of other boys and girls. Soon he noticed that she was tripping gaily back and forth, pretending to be busy chasing schoolmates, but each time she ran close by him. At last she said to a girl who was standing almost at Tom's elbow:

"Why, Mary Austin! You bad girl, why didn't you come to Sunday-school?"

"I did come—didn't you see me?"

"Why, no! Did you? Where did you sit?"

"I was in Miss Peters's class, where I always go. I saw you."

"Did you?" said Becky. "Why, it's funny I didn't see you. I wanted to tell you about the picnic."[1]

"Oh, that's jolly. Who's going to give it?"

"My mother is going to let me have one."

"Oh, goody; I hope she'll let me come."

"Well, she will. She'll let anybody come that I want, and I want you."

"That's ever so nice. When is it going to be?"

[1] picnic—a party in the open air

"Soon. When the holidays come."

"Oh, won't it be fun! Are you going to ask all the girls and boys?"

"Yes, every one that's friends with me—or wants to be," said Becky, glancing at Tom.

"Oh, may I come?" said Gracie Miller.

"Yes."

"And me?" said Sally Rogers.

"Yes."

"And me too?" said Susy Harper. "And my brother Joe?"

"Yes."

And so it went on, till all the group had asked to come except Tom and Amy Lawrence. Tom turned away, and took Amy with him. The tears came to Becky's eyes. She cared nothing about the picnic now. She went away into a corner, and had a good cry. But soon she stopped crying, and with an angry look in her eye, she tossed her head and said she knew what she would do.

At playtime Tom saw her sitting on a little bench, looking at a picture-book with Alfred Temple. They were so interested, and their heads were so close together over the book, that they took no notice of anybody else. Tom began to hate himself for not making friends with Becky, when she had given him the chance. He called himself a fool, and all the hard names he could think of. He was so angry that he wanted to cry. He could not help it.

"Any other boy!" Tom thought, grating his teeth. "Any boy in the whole town but that fellow who dresses so nicely. Oh, all right. I licked you the first day you ever saw this town, my lad, and I'll lick you again. You just wait till I catch you!"

Tom went straight home at noon. He could not put up with Amy any longer. Becky stayed at school, and went on looking at the picture-book with Alfred. But as the minutes dragged along, and no Tom came, she began to lose interest. She became very sad, and wished she had not been so unkind. Poor Alfred did his best to cheer her up, and kept on saying, "Oh, here's a jolly picture, look at this!" But Becky had seen enough of the pictures. "Oh, don't bother me!" she cried; "I don't care for them!" And bursting into tears, she got up and walked away.

Alfred followed, and tried to comfort her, but she said:

"Go away and leave me alone, can't you? I hate you!"

So the boy stopped, and wondered what he could have done to make her so cross. Then Alfred went sadly into the empty school-room. He was angry. He could see now that Becky had only been friendly with him so that she could make Tom Sawyer unhappy. He wished he could find a way to get that boy into trouble without much harm to himself.

He saw Tom's spelling-book on his desk. Here was his chance. He opened it, and poured ink over the pages. Becky glanced in through the window behind him, and saw what he was doing. She moved on, meaning to find Tom and tell him. Tom would be pleased, and they would be friends again. But soon she changed her mind. She remembered how he had taken no notice of her when she was talking about the picnic. So she decided to let him get whipped because of the messy spelling-book, and to hate him for ever.

After dinner, Tom set off for school and had the luck to meet Becky Thatcher in Meadow Lane. He ran up to her and said:

"I was very unkind to you this morning, Becky, and I'm so sorry. Will you be friends with me again?"

The girl stopped and looked him angrily in the face.

"I'll thank you to keep yourself *to* yourself, Mr. Thomas Sawyer," she said. "I'll never speak to you again."

She tossed her head and passed on. Poor girl, she did not know how fast she was nearing trouble.

The schoolmaster, Mr. Dobbins, kept a special book in his desk. Every day he took it out and looked at it when the class was working. He kept that book under lock and key. Every boy and girl in the school wanted to see it, but they never got the chance.

Now as Becky was passing by the desk, she noticed that the key was in the lock! She glanced around, found that she was alone, and the next minute she had the book in her hands. She began to turn the leaves, and was looking at one of the pictures, when Tom Sawyer stepped in at the door. Becky snatched at the book to close it, and was unlucky enough to tear the picture down the middle. She pushed the book into the desk, turned the key, and burst out crying.

"Tom Sawyer," she said, "you are just as mean as you can be, to creep up on a person and look at what they're looking at."

"How could *I* know you were looking at anything?" said Tom.

"You are wicked, Tom Sawyer. You are going to tell Mr. Dobbins what I have done; and, oh, what shall I do, what shall I do? I'll be whipped, and I have never been whipped in school before."

The she stamped her little foot and said:

"Tell him if you want to. I hate you!"

Tom did not know what to do.

"What a strange girl she is," he said to himself. "Never been licked! Shucks, what's a licking! That's just like a girl. Well, of course, I'm not going to tell old Dobbins about this little fool. But he will ask who it was that tore his book. Nobody will answer. Then he'll do what he always does—ask first one and then another, and when he comes to the right girl he'll know it. Girls' faces always give them away. She'll get licked, and it will serve her right."

In a short time the master came in, and the boys and girls went into the school-room. Soon Mr. Dobbins noticed the ink on Tom's spelling-book. Tom thought that he might have spilt the ink himself, and Becky did not say anything. "He'll tell about me tearing the picture," she said to herself. "I wouldn't say a word, not to save his life!" So Tom took his whipping, and went back to his seat.

A whole hour went by. The master sat sleepily in his chair. The class was hard at work. Presently Mr. Dobbins looked up, yawned, then unlocked his desk, took out the book, and began to read.

Tom glanced at Becky. She looked like a hunted rabbit.

At once he forgot his quarrel with her. Quick, something must be done! Should he snatch the book, spring through the door, and run? But it was too late. The master was standing up.

"Who tore this book?" he said.

There was not a sound. You could have heard a pin drop. Mr. Dobbins looked at each face.

"Benjamin Rogers, did you tear this book?"

"No, sir."

"Joseph Harper, did you?"

"No, sir."

"Amy Lawrence?"

Amy shook her head.

"Susan Harper, did you do this?"

"No, Mr. Dobbins."

The next girl was Becky Thatcher. Tom was shaking from head to foot.

"Rebecca Thatcher"—(Tom glanced at her face; it was white with terror)—"did you tear this book?"

A thought shot like lightning through Tom's brain. He jumped to his feet and shouted:

"*I* did it!"

Mr. Dobbins gave him a terrible whipping, but the surprise and thankfulness that shone upon him from poor Becky's eyes was enough to pay for a hundred whippings.

Tom was very happy when he went to bed that night. He fell asleep with Becky's last words ringing dreamily in his ear:

"Tom, how *could* you be so kind!"

Eight

At last the murder case came on in the court. Everybody in the village was talking about it. Tom could not get away from it. It kept him in a cold terror all the time. He took Huck to a lonely place to have a talk with him.

"Huck," he said, "have you ever told anybody about this?"

"About what?"

"You know what."

"*Oh*, of course I haven't."

"Never a word?"

"Not one word, so help me. What makes you ask?"

"Well, I was afraid."

"Why, Tom Sawyer, we wouldn't be alive two days if that got found out. *You* know that."

Tom felt more comfortable. Soon he said:

"Huck, nobody could make you tell, could they?"

"Make me tell? Why, if I wanted that half-breed devil to drown me they could make me tell. But there's no other way."

"Well, that's all right then. We're safe as long as we keep quiet."

There was silence for a few minutes, then Tom said:

"What is all the talk about, Huck?"

"Talk? Well, it's just Muff Potter, Muff Potter, Muff Potter all the time."

"I reckon he's finished," said Tom. "Don't you feel sorry for him sometimes?"

"Nearly always. He's no good, but then he has never done anything to hurt anybody. Just does a little fishing to get money for drink. But he's good. He gave me half a fish once, when there wasn't enough for two; and lots of times he's been kind to me when I was out of luck."

"Well, he's mended kites for me," said Tom. "I wish we could get him out of that prison."

"My, we couldn't get him out, Tom! And if we did, they'd catch him again."

The boys had a long talk, but it didn't make them feel any better. As the night drew on, they found themselves near the lonely little prison. They did as they had often done before—went to the window of the prison hut and gave Potter some tobacco and matches.

He was very thankful for their gifts. Huck and Tom felt awful when Potter said:

"You've been very good to me, boys—better than anybody else in this town. And I don't forget it, I don't. I often say to myself, 'I used to mend all the boys' kites and things, and show them the good fishing places, and now they've forgotten old Muff when he's in trouble. But Tom and Huck don't forget him, and I don't forget *them*!' Well, boys, I did an awful thing. I was very drunk at the time, I suppose. And now they're going to hang me."

Tom went home very unhappy, and his dreams that night were full of horrors. The next day and the day after, he hung about the room where the case was going on, longing to go in, but forcing himself to stay outside. It was just the same with Huck. They kept their ears open when people came out, but the news was always bad. At the end of the second day, when Injun Joe had told his story, everybody said that Muff Potter would be found guilty.

All the people of the village went to the court-house the next morning, for this was to be the great day. Potter had chains on him, and was made to stand where everybody could see him. Injun Joe was there. One man said that he saw Muff Potter washing in the river early on the morning when the murdered man was found, and that Potter crept away as soon as he was seen.

The next man to be asked questions told how he had found the knife near the dead body of Dr. Robinson.

A third man said that he had often seen the knife in Potter's hand.

Potter's lawyer did not ask him any questions. Everybody was surprised. Was Potter's lawyer going to throw his life away without trying to save him?

Some other people said how frightened Potter had looked when he was brought to the place where the murder had been done. Not one of them was asked any questions by Potter's lawyer.

Then the other lawyer said:

"We have now proved that the unhappy prisoner is guilty. We close our case here."

Poor Potter groaned, and he put his face in his hands, and rocked his body softly to and fro. There was silence. Many women were crying.

Potter's lawyer now rose and said:

"When this trial began I said that I would prove that the prisoner did this terrible murder while he was drunk. Now I have changed my mind." Then he said, "Call Thomas Sawyer."

Every eye was turned to Tom as he rose and took his place at the stand. The boy looked wild enough, for he was badly scared.

"Thomas Sawyer," said the lawyer, "where were you on the seventeenth of June, about the hour of midnight?"

Tom glanced at Injun Joe's cruel face, and he could not say a word. Everybody listened, but the words would not come. After a few minutes, however, the boy pulled himself together enough to speak.

"I was in the graveyard," he said.

"A little bit louder, please. Don't be afraid! You were . . ."

"In the graveyard."

There was a smile on the face of Injun Joe.

"Were you anywhere near Horse Williams's grave?"

"Yes, sir."

"Speak up just a little louder. How near were you?"

"As near as I am to you."

"Were you hidden or not?"

"I was hiding."

"Where?"

"Behind the trees on the edge of the grave."

Injun Joe gave a start.

"Was anyone with you?"

"Yes, sir. I went there with . . ."

"Wait—wait a minute. Do not tell us the name of your friend. We will hear him at the right time. Did you carry anything there with you?"

Tom did not reply.

"Speak out, my boy," said the lawyer. "It is always best to tell the truth. What did you take there?"

"Only a—a—dead cat."

Everybody laughed, and the judge called for silence.

"We will show the body of that cat," said the lawyer. "Now, my boy, tell us everything that happened—tell it in your own way. Don't miss out anything, and don't be afraid."

Tom began. He told them all that he had seen that night, and when he said, "And as the doctor swung the board and knocked Muff Potter down, Injun Joe jumped with the knife and . . ."

Crash! Quick as lightning Injun Joe sprang for a window, tore his way through all who tried to stop him, and was gone!

Tom was quite a hero now. His name was printed in the newspaper. There were some who said that he would be President of the United States yet, if they did not hang him first.

Tom was happy during the day, but his nights were full of horror. He never went out in the dark. Poor Huck was just as frightened, for Tom had told the whole story to Potter's lawyer the night before the great day of the trial, and Huck was frightened that the part he had taken in it all might be told. Muff Potter was so thankful that Tom was glad he had spoken, but he was afraid that Injun Joe would never be caught. Money had been offered, and people had looked everywhere. But no Injun Joe was found. Tom felt sure he could never be safe again until that man was dead and he had seen the corpse.

Nine

There comes a time in the life of every boy when he wants very much to go somewhere and dig for hidden treasure. Tom suddenly felt like this one day. He set out to tell Joe Harper, but could not find him. Next he looked for Ben Rogers; he had gone fishing. Presently he met Huck Finn. Huck would do. Tom took him to a lonely place and told him about his plans. Huck was willing.

"Where shall we dig?" said Huck.

"Oh, almost anywhere."

"Why, is it hidden all around?"

"No, indeed it isn't. Treasure's hidden in very special places, Huck—sometimes on islands, sometimes in old boxes under an old dead tree; but mostly under the floor in haunted houses."[1]

"Who hides it?" asked Huck.

"Why, robbers, of course—who do you think? Sunday-school teachers?"

"I don't know. If it was mine I wouldn't hide it: I'd spend it and have a good time."

"So would I; but robbers don't do that. They always hide it and leave it there."

"Don't they come back for it?"

[1] haunted house—a lonely house in which there are ghosts

"No. They think they will, but they usually forget where they put it, or else they die."

"How are you going to find the hiding-place?" said Huck.

"They always bury it under a haunted house, or on an island, or under a dead tree. We can try Jackson's Island some time; and there's the old haunted house up the Still-House brook, and there's lots of dead trees."

"Is it under all of them?"

"How silly you talk! No!"

"Then how are you going to know which one to go for?"

"Go for all of them," said Tom.

"Why, that would take all summer."

"Well, what does it matter? Suppose you find a pot with a hundred dollars in it, or an old box full of diamonds. How's that?"

Huck's eyes brightened.

"That's fine. Just you give me the hundred dollars, and I don't want any diamonds."

"All right. But *I* should like some diamonds. Some of them are worth twenty dollars each."

"No! Is that so?" said Huck.

"Oh yes. Anybody will tell you so. Have you never seen one, Huck?"

"Not that I remember."

"Oh, kings have loads of them."

"Well, I don't know any kings, Huck."

"I know you don't. But if you went to Europe you would see plenty of them hopping around."

"Do they hop?" asked Huck.

"Hop?—your grandmother! No!"

"Well, why did you say they did?"

"Shucks! I only meant you would *see* them—not hopping, of course—what do they want to hop for? But I mean you would just see them—all over the place, you know."

"All right," said Huck. "Where shall we dig first?"

"Well, I don't know. Suppose we go to the old tree on the hill, on the other side of Still-House brook?"

"Yes."

So they got an old pick and a shovel, and set out on their three-mile walk. They got there hot and breathless, and threw themselves down in the shade of an oak tree to rest and have a smoke.

"I like this," said Tom.

"So do I."

"Say, Huck, if we find a treasure here, what will you do with your share?"

"Well, I'll have a pie and an ice-cream every day, and I'll go to every circus that comes along. I'll bet I'll have a fine time. What will you do with *your* share?"

"I'm going to buy a new drum," said Tom, "and a sword, and a red tie, and a bull pup, and get married."

"Oh, Tom, if you get married I shall be all alone."

"No, you won't. You can come and live with me. Now come along, and we'll start digging."

They worked and sweated for half an hour, but found nothing. They dug for another half hour. Still there was nothing. At last Huck said:

"Do they always bury it as deep as this?"

"Sometimes—not always. Perhaps we have got the wrong place."

So they chose a new spot and began again. They were

getting tired, and soon Huck wiped his face with his sleeve and said:

"Where are you going to dig next, after we get this one?"

"Under the old tree on Cardiff Hill, behind the widow's cottage."

The work went on. By-and-by Huck said:

"I think we must be in the wrong place again. What do you think?"

"It's very strange, Huck. I don't understand it. Say, let's try the haunted house."

"I don't like haunted houses, Tom, but we'll try it if you say so."

They started off. Soon they saw the "haunted" house in the middle of the valley. Its fences had gone long ago. The chimney had fallen in. The windows were broken, and a corner of the roof had gone. The boys looked at it for a time, and then began to make their way home through the woods.

On Saturday, shortly after noon, the two boys took their tools and went back to the haunted house. They crept to the door and peeped in. They saw a room full of weeds, an old fireplace, broken windows, and a broken-down staircase. There were cobwebs everywhere. They went in quietly, talking in whispers, threw their tools into a corner, and made their way upstairs. They looked round, and were getting ready to go down again and begin work when . . .

"Sh!" said Tom.

"What is it?" whispered Huck, growing white.

"Sh! There! Do you hear it?"

"Yes! Oh my! Let's run!" whispered Huck.

"Keep still! Don't you move! They are coming right towards the door."

The boys lay down on the floor with their eyes to the holes in the boards and waited full of fear.

"They have stopped—No—they are coming! Here they are. Don't whisper another word, Huck. My goodness, I wish I was out of this!"

Two men came in. Each boy said to himself:

"There's the old deaf and dumb Spaniard that has been about the town once or twice lately—never saw the other before."

"The other" was a ragged fellow with a cruel face. The Spaniard was wearing a long overcoat; he had bushy white whiskers, white hair showed under his hat, and he wore green glasses. When they came in, "the other" was talking in a low voice. They sat down on the ground, facing the door, and the speaker said:

"No, I've thought it all over, and I don't like it. It's dangerous."

"Dangerous?" grunted the "deaf and dumb" Spaniard, to the surprise of the boys. "Milksop!"

This voice made the boys jump. It was Injun Joe's! There was silence for some time; then Joe said:

"Look here, lad, you go back up the river. Wait till you hear from me. I'll go into the town just once more, for a look. We'll rob that house after I've spied round a little. Then off we go to Texas! We'll go together!"

"All right."

"What shall we do with the money we stole the other day?" said Joe.

"I don't know. Leave it here as we've always done, I reckon. It's too heavy to carry."

"Then we'll bury it—and bury it deep."

"Good idea," said the comrade, who walked across the room, knelt down, lifted a stone from near the fireplace, and took out a bag that jingled pleasantly. He took from it twenty or thirty dollars, and passed the bag to Injun Joe, who was on his knees in the corner, now, digging with his knife.

The boys forgot all their fears. With hungry eyes they watched every movement.

Joe's knife struck upon something.

"Hello!" said he.

"What is it?" said his comrade.

"It's a box. Here, help me, and we'll see what it is. Never mind, I've broken a hole in it."

He put his hand in, and drew it out.

"Man, it's money!"

The two men gazed at the coins. They were gold. The boys were as excited as themselves.

Joe's friend said:

"We'll make quick work of this. There's an old rusty pick over amongst the weeds in the corner—I saw it a minute ago."

He ran and brought the boys' pick and shovel. Injun Joe took the pick, looked at it carefully, shook his head, said something quietly to himself, and then began to use it.

The box was soon uncovered. It was not very large. The men looked at the treasure it contained in silence.

"There's hundreds of dollars here," said Injun Joe.

"They always said that Murrel's gang came here," said the other.

"I know that," said Injun Joe. "They must have buried this before they left."

"Now you won't need to do that job."

The half-breed looked thoughtful. Said he:

"You don't know me. It isn't robbery altogether—it's revenge!"[1] A wicked light flamed in his eyes. "I shall need your help. When it's finished—then Texas. Go home, and wait till you hear from me."

"Well, I will if you say so. What shall we do with this—bury it again?"

"No!" said Injun Joe. "That pick had fresh earth on it!" (The boys were sick with terror when they heard this.) "What are the pick and shovel doing here? Why have they fresh earth on them? Who brought them here—and where have they gone? Have you heard anybody—seen anybody? What! Bury it again, and leave them to come and find it? No! We'll take it to my den."

"Why, of course. I might have thought about that before. You mean number one?"

"No—number two—under the cross. The other place is not safe."

"All right. It's nearly dark enough to start."

Injun Joe got up and crept to the window. Soon he said:

"Who could have brought those tools here? Do you think they can be upstairs?"

The boys held their breath. Injun Joe put his hand on his knife, and turned towards the stairs. He crept slowly up, and the lads were about to spring through the window, when there was a crash, and Injun Joe

[1] revenge—something wicked which is done to get one's own back

landed on the ground beneath the fallen staircase. He got up angrily, and his friend said:

"Now what's the use of all that? If there is anybody up there, let them stay—who cares? It will be dark in fifteen minutes—and then let them follow us if they want to."

Joe grumbled for a time; then he agreed with his

friend that they ought to be leaving. Soon afterwards they slipped out of the house, and moved towards the river carefully carrying the box.

Tom and Huck got up, and looked after them through the holes between the logs of the house. Should they follow? Not they—they were glad to reach the ground again without broken necks and make their way home.

They said to each other they would keep a look-out for that Spaniard when he came to town, and follow him to "number two", whatever that might be. Then a terrible thought struck Tom:

"Revenge? What if he means *us*, Huck!"

"Oh, don't," said Huck.

They talked it all over, and as they came into the town they both thought that he might mean somebody else.

Ten

The next morning Tom found Huck sitting on the edge of a boat, idly swinging his feet in the water, and looking very sad. He said :

"Hello, Huck!"

"Hello yourself."

There was silence for a minute, and then Huck said :

"Tom, if we had left those tools at the dead tree, we could have got the money. Oh, it's awful!"

"It wasn't a dream, then, it wasn't a dream! Somehow, I almost wish it was."

"What isn't a dream?"

"Oh, what happened yesterday."

"Dream! I've been dreaming of that Spanish devil all night, rot him!"

"No, not rot him. Find him! Track the money!"

"Tom, we shall never find him. A fellow only has one chance to get a treasure like that, and we've lost it. I should feel very frightened if I saw him, anyway."

"Well, so would I; but I'd like to see him, and track him to his number two."

"Number two; yes, that's it. I've been thinking about that, but I can't understand it. What can it be?"

"Perhaps it's the number of a room—in an inn, you know!"

"Oh, that's it! There are only two inns in the town. We can soon find out."

"You stay here Huck, till I come back."

Tom ran off at once. He was gone half an hour. He found that in the best inn a young lawyer was living in number two. At the other inn, Tom could not find out who was living in number two. The inn-keeper's young son said it was kept locked all the time, and he never saw anybody go into it or come out of it except at night.

"That's what I've found out, Huck," said Tom, when he came back. "That must be the number two we want."

"I reckon it is, Tom. Now what are you going to do?"

"Let me think."

Tom thought for a long time. Then he said :

"I'll tell you. The back door of that number two comes out into the little lane between the inn and the brick-store. Now you get hold of all the keys you can. I'll take auntie's keys, and the first dark night we'll go there and try them. And keep a look-out for Injun Joe. If you see him, you just follow him. If he doesn't go to that number two, it isn't the place."

"Lordy, I don't want to follow him by myself!"

"It will be dark. He may never see you. I'll follow him if it's dark. Why, he may be going right back for that money."

That night Tom and Huck were ready for their adventure. They waited near the inn till nearly nine. Nobody came into the lane or left it. Nobody looking like a Spaniard came near the inn. The night was fine and clear, so Tom went home. Huck promised to come and "miaow" if it got dark, and they would then return and try the keys. But the night remained clear, and about twelve, Huck went to sleep in an empty sugar barrel.

On Tuesday the boys had the same bad luck. Also Wednesday. But Thursday night was better. Tom slipped out in good time with his aunt's old tin lantern, which he hid in Huck's barrel. They began to watch. An hour before midnight the inn closed, and its lights were put out. No Spaniard had been seen. Nobody had been near the lane. Everything was quiet. The night was dark, and there was thunder in the distance.

Tom got his lantern, lit it inside the barrel, covered it in a towel, and the two boys crept towards the inn. Huck kept watch and Tom felt his way into the lane. Huck waited. He began to wish he could see a flash from the lantern—it would frighten him, but it would tell him that Tom was still alive.

It seemed hours since Tom had gone. Surely something must have happened; perhaps he was dead. Suddenly there was a flash of light, and Tom came racing past.

"Run!" said he; "run for your life!"

There was no need for him to shout twice; once was enough. Huck was already making thirty or forty miles an hour. The boys didn't stop till they reached an old shed at the lower end of the village. Just as they got inside the storm burst and the rain poured down. As soon as Tom got his breath he said:

"Huck, it was awful! I tried two of the keys as gently as I could, but they seemed to make such a noise that I could hardly breathe, I was so scared. They wouldn't turn in the lock either. Well, without noticing what I was doing, I took hold of the knob, and the door came open! It wasn't locked! I hopped in and shook the towel off the lantern, and *great Caesar's ghost!*"

"What!—what did you see, Tom?"

"Huck, I almost stepped on to Injun Joe's hand!"

"No!"

"Yes. He was lying there, sound asleep on the floor, with his arms spread out."

"Lordy, what did you do? Did he wake up?"

"No, never moved. He was drunk, I think. I just snatched that towel and ran!"

"I should never have thought of the towel," said Huck.

"Well, I did. My aunt would be very cross if I lost it."

"Say, Tom, did you see that box?"

"Huck, I didn't wait to look around. I didn't see the box. I didn't see the cross. I didn't see anything but a bottle and a tin cup on the floor by Injun Joe."

"If Injun Joe is drunk," said Huck, "this is a good time to get the box."

"Well, you try it!" replied Tom.

Huck seemed to think better of it.

"Well, no—I reckon not."

There was a long pause, and then Tom said:

"Look here, Huck, we won't try again till we know that Injun Joe is not in there. It's too dangerous. Now if we watch every night, we'll be sure to see him go out some time or other, and then we can snatch the box as quick as lightning."

"Well," said Huck, "all right. I'll watch the whole

night long, and I'll do it every night too, if you will do the other part of the job."

"All right, I will. All you have to do is to trot up to my house and miaow—and if I'm asleep, throw some stones at the window. That will fetch me."

"Agreed."

"Now, Huck, the storm is over, and I'll go home. It will be day-light in a couple of hours. You go back and watch till then, will you?"

"I said I would, Tom, and I will. I'll watch that inn for a year. I'll sleep all day and I'll watch all night."

"That's all right. Now where are you going to sleep?"

"In Ben Rogers's hay-loft."

"Well," said Tom, "if I don't want you in the day-time, Huck, I'll let you sleep. Any time you see something in the night, just skip around and miaow."

Eleven

The first thing Tom heard on Friday morning was a piece of good news. Becky Thatcher's mother was going to let her have the picnic the next day. All the invitations were sent out before sunset, and the young people of the village began to get ready. Tom was so excited that he stayed awake quite late that night. He was hoping to hear Huck's "miaow", and to have the treasure so that he could surprise Becky the next day; but he was disappointed. No signal came that night.

Morning came at last, and by ten or eleven o'clock the happy crowd was ready to start. They were going to travel down the river in the old steam ferry-boat, and soon they were making their way up the main street with their baskets of food. Sid was sick and had to miss the fun; cousin Mary stayed at home to keep him company. The last thing Mrs. Thatcher said to Becky was:

"You won't get back till late. Perhaps you had better stay all night with some of the girls that live near the ferry landing, child."

"Then I'll stay with Susy Harper, mamma."

"Very well. And mind, be a good girl, and don't be any trouble."

Soon, as they walked along, Tom said to Becky:

"Say—I'll tell you what we'll do. Instead of going to Susy Harper's house, we'll climb right up the hill and stay with Widow Douglas. She'll have ice-cream! She has it almost every day—loads of it. And she'll be awfully glad to have us."

"Oh, that will be fun!" cried Becky. "But what will mamma say?"

"How will she ever know?"

Then Becky thought a moment, and said:

"I reckon it's wrong—but . . ."

"But; shucks!" said Tom. "Your mother won't know, and so what's the harm? She only wants you to be safe."

The thought of Widow Douglas and her ice-cream was so nice they decided to stay with her, but not to tell anybody about this change of plan.

Three miles below the town the ferry-boat stopped

at the mouth of a woody hollow. The crowd of boys and girls went ashore, and soon they were shouting and laughing in the forest and on the hills. Then they ate their food, and after that they rested in the shade of the trees. After a while, somebody shouted :

"Who is ready for the caves?"

Everybody was. They took some candles, and went running up the hill. The mouth of the cave was high up on the hillside, an opening shaped like the letter A. Its heavy wooden door was open. They lit their candles and began to wander down the steep slope. This part of the cave was not more than eight or ten feet wide. Every few steps there were narrower paths leading to smaller caves which ran into each other and out again. You could wander for days and nights, going down and down into the earth, and never find the end. No one knew his way through. That was impossible. Most of the young men knew part of it, but they never went in very far. Tom Sawyer knew as much as any one.

The boys and girls moved along the main track for about three-quarters of a mile, and then little groups began to slip aside into the smaller caves. Soon, one group after another came back to the mouth of the main cave, covered with clay, and feeling very happy with the success of the day. They were astonished to find that they had been taking no note of time, and that it was beginning to get dark. The bell had been calling for half an hour. When the ferry-boat pushed into the stream, nobody but the captain cared sixpence for the wasted time.

Huck was already upon his watch when the ferry-boat's lights went past. The night was growing cloudy and dark. Ten o'clock came, and the lights of the village began to wink out. Eleven o'clock came. The lights of the inn were put out. There was darkness everywhere, now. Huck waited a long time, but nothing happened. Was it any use? Why not give it up and turn in?

A noise fell upon his ear. A door closed softly. He sprang to the corner of the brick-store. The next moment two men brushed by him, and one seemed to have something under his arm. It must be that box! So they were going to remove the treasure. Why call Tom now? It would be silly—the men would get away with the box and never be found again. No, he would follow them. So Huck stepped out and crept along behind the men like a cat.

They went up the main street, then turned to the left up a cross street. They went straight ahead, then, until they came to the path that led up Cardiff Hill; this they took. They passed by the old Welshman's house, half way up the hill, and still went on climbing. Good, thought Huck, they will bury the treasure in the old quarry.[1] But they never stopped at the quarry. They passed on up a narrow path, and were at once hidden in the darkness.

Huck walked quickly, then stopped. No sound; none, except that he seemed to hear the beating of his own heart. The hoot of an owl came from over the hill. But no footsteps. Heavens, was everything lost? He was about to spring forward, when a man coughed, not four feet from him! Huck's heart sprang into his throat, and he stood there shaking. He knew where he was. He

[1] quarry—place where stone is dug out from the hill

knew he was near the garden of the Widow Douglas. "Very well," he thought, "let them bury it there; it won't be hard to find."

Now there was a low voice—a very low voice—Injun Joe's:

"Drat her, maybe she's got company—the lights are on, late as it is."

"I can't see any."

This was the stranger's voice—the stranger of the haunted house. A deadly chill went to Huck's heart—this, then, was the "revenge" job! He remembered that the Widow Douglas had been kind to him more than once, and perhaps these men were going to murder her. He wished he could talk to her; but he didn't dare—they might come and catch him. Soon he heard Injun Joe say:

"You can't see the lights because the bush is in the way. Now—move over here. You see now, don't you?"

"Yes. There must be somebody with her. Better give it up."

"Give it up," whispered Injun Joe, "just as I'm leaving the country for ever! Give it up, and perhaps never have another chance. I tell you I don't care for her money—you can have that. But her husband was rough on me—many times he was rough on me. He had me put in prison. And that isn't all! He had me whipped, with all the town looking on. Whipped—do you understand? He died, but I'll have my revenge on *her*!"

"Oh, don't kill her! Don't do that!"

"Kill? Who said anything about killing? I would kill him if he was here; but not her. When you want to get revenge on a woman you don't kill her. You spoil her looks. You cut her face."

"But that's terrible! that's . . ."

"Be quiet. It will be safest for you. I'll tie her to the bed. If she bleeds to death, I can't help that. My friend, you are going to help me! If you don't, I'll kill you."

"Well," replied the stranger, "if it's got to be done, let's start. The quicker the better—I'm all in a shiver."

"Do it now?—and company there? No—we'll wait till the lights are out—there's no hurry."

Huck held his breath. He took a step back, and listened. There was no sound. All was still. He turned in his tracks, and began to creep along as quietly as he could. When he reached the quarry he felt safe, so he took to his heels and ran. Down, down he ran till he reached the Welshman's house. He banged at the door, and soon the old man and his two sons looked out through the windows.

"What's the row there? Who's banging? What do you want?"

"Let me in—quick!" cried Huck. "I'll tell everything."

"Why, who are you?"

"Huckleberry Finn—quick, let me in!"

"Let him in, lads," cried the Welshman, "and let's see what's the trouble."

"Please don't ever tell I told you," were Huck's first words when he got in. "Please don't—I'd be killed—but the widow's been a good friend to me, and I want to tell."

"By George, he has got something to tell, or he

wouldn't act like this!" said the old man. "Out with it, lad. Nobody here will tell."

Three minutes later the old man and his sons, with their guns in their hands, were up the hill and going along the path on tiptoe. Huck followed them no farther. He hid behind a rock, and listened. There was a long silence, and then he heard the sound of a shot and a cry. He sprang away and tore down the hill as fast as his legs would carry him.

Twelve

As soon as dawn came on Sunday morning, Huck went up the hill and knocked gently on the Welshman's door. A call came from a window:

"Who's there?"

Huck's scared voice answered in a low tone:

"Do please let me in! It's only Huck Finn!"

The door was quickly unlocked and he went in. Huck was given a seat, and the old man and his tall sons dressed themselves.

"Now, my boy, I hope you're good and hungry, because breakfast will be ready as soon as the sun's up, and we'll have a nice hot one, too. The boys and I hoped you'd turn up and stop here last night."

"I was awfully scared," said Huck, "and I ran. I didn't stop for three miles. I've come now because I want to know about it; and I'm here before day-light because I don't want to meet those devils, even if they were dead."

"Well, poor chap, you do look as if you'd had a hard night—but there's a bed for you when you've had your breakfast. No, they're not dead—we are sorry for that. You see, we knew where to put our hands on them, so we crept along on tiptoe till we got within fifteen feet of them—dark as night that path was—and just then I found I was going to sneeze.

"When they heard the sneeze, the two men started to run. 'Fire!' I cried, and blazed away. So did the boys. But they were off through the woods, and we lost them. Then we went down and called up the police. As soon as it is light they are going to hunt in the woods with the sheriff. You couldn't see what the men looked like in the dark, lad, I suppose?"

"Oh, yes," replied Huck. "I saw them in the town and followed them. One is the old deaf and dumb Spaniard that's been around here once or twice, and the other is a thin, ragged . . ."

"That's enough, lad, we know the men. Met them in the woods behind the widow's house one day, and they crept away. Off with you, boys, and tell the sheriff!"

The Welshman's sons left at once. As they were going, Huck sprang up and said:

"Oh, please don't say that I told you about them. Oh, please!"

Everybody was early at church that day. The news had spread through the town. There was still no sign of the two men. When the sermon was finished Judge Thatcher's wife went up to Mrs. Harper and said:

"Is my Becky going to sleep all day? I knew she would be tired."

"Your Becky?"

"Yes," replied Mrs. Thatcher, with a startled look. "Didn't she stay with you last night?"

"Why, no."

Mrs. Thatcher turned white, and sank into a seat just as Aunt Polly passed by. Aunt Polly said:

"Good morning, Mrs. Thatcher. Good morning,

Mrs. Harper. My boy is missing. I think my Tom must have stayed with one of you last night. And now he's afraid to come to church. I am very cross with him."

Mrs. Thatcher shook her head, and turned still whiter.

"He didn't stay with us," said Mrs. Harper, beginning to look uneasy.

"Joe Harper," said Aunt Polly, "have you seen my Tom this morning?"

"No, mam."

"When did you see him last?"

Joe tried to remember, but was not sure he could say. The people had stopped moving out of church. Whispers passed along. Children were questioned. They all said they had not noticed whether Tom and Becky were on board the ferry-boat on the homeward trip. It was dark, and no one thought of asking if any one was missing. At last one young man said he feared they were still in the cave! Mrs. Thatcher fainted, and Aunt Polly began to cry.

The alarm went from lip to lip, from group to group, from street to street. Within five minutes the bells were wildly ringing, and the whole town was up. The burglars were forgotten. Horses were saddled; the ferry-boat was ordered out; and soon two hundred men were pouring down the high-road and river towards the cave.

All the long afternoon the village seemed empty and dead. Many women visited Aunt Polly and Mrs. Thatcher, and tried to comfort them. They cried with them, too, and that was better than words.

All that night the town waited for news: but when

the morning dawned at last, all the word that came was, "Send more candles, and send food." The old Welshman came home towards day-light, covered with candle-grease and clay, and almost worn out. He found Huck still in bed, but he was now ill. The doctors were all at the cave, so the Widow Douglas came to look after the sick boy.

Early in the morning parties of weary men began to come back into the village, but the strongest went on looking. In one place, deep in the caves, the names "BECKY" and "TOM" had been found written on the rocky wall with candle smoke. Some said that now and then a far-away spot of light would be seen—but the children were not there; it was only the light of somebody looking.

Three terrible days and nights dragged along. The village began to give up hope, for the missing children could not be found.

We must now return to Tom and Becky. On the day of the picnic they went along the dark passages with the other children. Then they went off down a twisting side-track, holding up their candles, and reading the names that had been written on the walls with candle smoke. Still walking along together and talking, they did not really notice that they were now in a part of the cave where there were no marks on the walls. They smoked their own names, and moved on. At last they began to grow tired, and Becky said :

"Why, I didn't notice; but it seems ever so long since I heard any of the others. I wonder how long we have been down here, Tom? Do you think we ought to go back?"

"Perhaps we should," said Tom.

"Can you find the way? I hope we won't get lost. It would be so awful!"

They started off, hurrying their steps. Tom shouted. The sound of his call died out in the distance like laughter.

"Oh, don't do it again, Tom, it is too horrid," said Becky.

"It *is* horrid, Becky," replied Tom; "but they *might* hear us, you know."

He shouted again. They stood still and listened, but they could hear no answering shout. They moved on again.

"Becky," said Tom at last, "I can't find the way. It's all mixed up."

"Tom, Tom," cried Becky. "We're lost, we're lost! We never, never can get out of this awful place! Oh, why did we ever leave the others?"

She sank to the ground and burst out crying. Tom sat down by her side and put his arms round her. He begged her to have a little hope, and she said she could not. But she got up and followed him until she grew so tired that she could go no farther. She sat down. Tom rested with her, and they talked of home, and the friends there, and the nice beds and above all, the light! Soon Becky fell asleep. Tom was glad, and as she slept he tried to think what he should do.

Suddenly he had a thought. There were some side-passages near at hand. It would be better to try some of these than pass the time doing nothing. He took a kite-line from his pocket and tied it to a rock. When Becky woke up they started off. Tom led the way, unwinding the line as they moved along.

They had gone only a few steps when Tom saw a man's hand, holding a candle, appear behind a rock. He shouted for joy, and instantly the hand was followed by the body it belonged to—the body of Injun Joe! Tom could not move. He was very glad the next moment to see the "Spaniard" take to his heels and rush out of sight. Becky had seen nothing of this, and Tom told her that he had only shouted "for luck".

The children sat down again. They were very hungry, and soon they fell asleep. After what seemed a very long time they woke up and began to move slowly forward. Tom decided to try another passage, but Becky was now too weak to go with him. She said she would wait where she was, and die—it would not be long. Tom kissed her; then he took the kite-line in his hand and went groping down one of the passages on his hands and knees.

Thirteen

Tuesday afternoon came, and the village of St. Petersburg was full of sadness. The lost children had not been found. Prayers had been said for them in the church, but still no good news came from the cave. Mrs. Thatcher was very ill. People said it broke their hearts to hear her calling for her child. Aunt Polly's grey hair had grown almost white. The villagers went to bed that night sad and hopeless.

In the middle of the night, however, a wild ringing burst from the bells, and in a minute the streets were full of people, who shouted, "Turn out! Turn out! They're found! They're found!" Tin pans and horns added to the noise, and soon everybody was moving down to the river. They met the children coming along in an open carriage drawn by shouting men and women who were sweeping up the main street shouting hurrah after hurrah.

All the lights in the village were put on. Nobody went to bed again. It was the greatest night the little town had ever seen.

Tom lay upon a sofa and told the story of his wonderful adventure. He had gone down one of the passages as far as his kite-line would reach, and was going to turn back when he saw far-off what looked like a patch of day-light. He dropped the line and made his way towards it. Then pushing his head and shoulders through a small hole, he saw the broad river rolling by! And if it had been night, he would not have seen that speck of day-light, and would not have explored that passage any more!

He said how he went back for Becky and told her the good news. She jumped for joy when she saw the day-light. Tom pushed his way out of the hole, and then helped Becky out. They sat there and cried, because they were so glad. At last, some men came along in a rowing boat, took them to a house, and gave them supper before bringing them home.

In two or three days the children were quite well again. Tom heard that Huck was ill and went to see him on Friday. He was told what had happened at Cardiff Hill. The body of the ragged man had been found in the river; he must have been drowned while trying to get away.

About a fortnight later, when Huck was quite better, Tom set off to visit him. Judge Thatcher's house was on the way, so he called in to see Becky. The judge asked him, jokingly, if he would like to go to the cave again. Tom said yes, he thought he wouldn't mind.

"Well," said the judge, "nobody will get lost in that cave any more. I've had its big door covered with iron and locked; and I have the key."

Tom turned as white as a sheet.

"What's the matter, boy?" cried the judge. "Here, run, somebody! Fetch a glass of water!"

The water was brought and thrown into Tom's face.

"Ah, now you're all right," said the judge. "What was the matter with you, Tom?"

"Oh, Judge, Injun Joe is in the cave!"

Within a few minutes the news spread, and many boats full of men were on their way to the cave. Tom Sawyer was in the boat that carried Judge Thatcher. When the cave door was unlocked, they saw Injun Joe lying on the ground, dead, with his face close to the crack of the door. The poor fellow had starved [1] to death. He was buried near the mouth of the cave.

The morning after he was buried, Tom took Huck to a lonely place to have a talk. He said:

"Huck, that money was never in the inn!"

"What!" said Huck, looking at his friend hard. "Tom, have you got on the track of that money again?"

"Huck, it's in the cave!"

Huck's eyes blazed.

"Say it again, Tom!"

"The money is in the cave! Will you go there with me and help to get it out?"

"You bet I will, if we can find it and not get lost."

"Huck, we can do it without the least little bit of trouble."

"Good! What makes you think the money is . . ."

"Huck, you just wait till we get in there. If we don't find it, I'll give you my drum, and everything I've got in the world."

"All right. When shall we start?"

"Right now, if you're ready."

A little after noon the boys got out a rowing boat and

---

[1] to starve—to die from having no food

set off down the river. When they were some miles below "Cave Hollow", Tom said:

"Do you see that white place up there? Well, that's one of my marks. We'll get ashore now."

They landed.

"Now, Huck," said Tom, "where we're standing, you could touch the hole I got out of with a fishing-pole. See if you can find it."

Huck tried, but found nothing. Pleased with himself, Tom marched into some bushes and said:

"Here you are! Look at it, Huck; it's the finest hole in this country. You just keep quiet about it. I've always wanted to be a robber, but I knew I must have a hiding-place like this first. Well, we've got one now, and we'll keep quiet about it, only we'll tell Joe Harper and Ben Rogers—because there's got to be a gang. Tom Sawyer's Gang—it sounds good, doesn't it?"

"Well, it just does, Tom. But who shall we rob?"

"Oh, almost anybody."

"And kill them?"

"No—not always. Keep them in the cave till they pay a ransom!"

"What's a ransom?"

"Money. You make them get all they can from their friends, and after you've kept them shut up for a year, if it isn't paid, you kill them. That's the usual way. Only you don't kill the women. You take their watches and things, but you always take your hat off and talk politely. Nobody is as polite as a robber—you'll see that in any book."

"Why, it's fine, Tom. I think it's better than being a pirate."

By this time everything was ready and the boys climbed into the hole, Tom in the lead. They made their way to the end of the tunnel, then they tied their kite-strings to a rock and moved on. Soon Tom whispered:

"Now, I'll show you something, Huck. Look as far round that corner as you can. Do you see that? There— on the big rock—done with candle-smoke."

"Tom, it's a *cross*!"

"Now where's your number two? '*Under the cross*', hey? That's where I saw Injun Joe poke up his candle, Huck. We'll go down there and hunt for the box."

Tom went first. Huck followed. In a small opening they found blankets, some bits of bacon, and the bones of two or three fowls. But there was no money-box. They searched everywhere, but in vain. Tom said:

"He said *under* the cross. Look, there's footprints

and some candle on the clay at one side of this rock, but not on the other sides. Now what's that for? I bet you the money *is* under the rock. I'm going to dig in the clay."

He got out his knife, and had not dug four inches before he struck wood.

"Hey, Hucky, do you hear that?"

Huck began to dig and scratch now. Some boards were soon uncovered and taken out. Beneath them was a hole which led under the rock. Tom got in, and a minute later he shouted:

"My goodness, Huck, look here!"

It was the treasure-box, sure enough.

"Got it at last!" said Huck, dipping his hands in the coins. "My, but we're rich, Tom! Let's get out of here!"

The money was soon in the bags that the boys had brought with them. They climbed out of the hole, put the money in their boat, and were soon racing along towards home. They landed shortly after dark.

"Now, Huck," said Tom, "we'll hide the money in the loft of the widow's wood-shed. You stay here and watch the stuff while I run and get Benny Taylor's little cart. I won't be gone a minute."

He ran off, and soon came back with the cart. They put the bags of money into it, threw some old rags on top, and started off. When the boys reached the Welshman's house they stopped to rest. Just as they were about to move on, the Welshman stepped out and said:

"Hello, who's that?"

"Huck Finn and Tom Sawyer, Mr. Jones."

"Good! Come along with me, boys, you are keeping everybody waiting. Hurry up; I'll pull the cart for you.

Why, it's quite heavy. Have you got bricks in it, or old metal?"

"Old metal," said Tom.

"I thought so. Hurry along, hurry along!"

Soon the boys were being pushed into the drawing-room of the Widow Douglas. Mr. Jones left the cart near the door, and followed them. All the important people of the village were there, dressed in their best clothes. The boys were covered with clay and candle, and Aunt Polly looked cross and shook her head at Tom. Mrs. Douglas took them to a bedroom, and said:

"Now wash and dress yourselves. Here are two new suits—shirts, socks, and everything. Get into them. We'll wait—come down when you are clean."

Then she left.

Fourteen

Huck said:

"Tom, we can get out of this if we can find a rope. The window isn't high from the ground."

"Shucks! What do you want to get out for?"

"Well, I'm not used to that kind of a crowd. I can't stand it. I'm not going down there, Tom."

"Oh, it isn't anything. I don't mind a bit. I'll take care of you."

Sid came into the room.

"Now, Sid," said Tom, "what is all this about?"

"The widow is giving a party," said Sid. "It's for the Welshman and his sons, because they helped her the other night. And I can tell you something else, if you want to know."

"Well, what?" said Tom.

"Why, old Mr. Jones is going to tell everybody how Huck tracked the robbers to the widow's house. I heard him saying this to Aunt Polly."

Some minutes later they were all sitting at the supper-table. At the proper time Mr. Jones made his little speech, thanking the widow for being so good to him—and then he spoke of Huck's share in the adventure. The widow was so thankful that she said she would give Huck a home in her own house, and that when she could spare the money she would start him in business. Tom said:

"Huck doesn't need it. Huck's rich! He has lots of money. Oh, you need not smile. I can show you. You just wait a minute!"

Tom ran out of doors. Soon he came back, bent under the weight of the heavy bags. He poured the yellow coins on to the table, and said:

"There—what did I tell you? Half of it belongs to Huck, and half to me!"

Everybody gazed. Nobody spoke for a moment. Then they all wanted to know where all this money had come from. Tom told them everything.

The money was counted. It was more than twelve thousand dollars.

You may be sure that the boys' good fortune made a great stir in the poor little village of St. Petersburg. Nobody had ever seen so much money before. Every "haunted" house was pulled apart, plank by plank, in the search for more hidden treasure, but nothing was found. The Widow Douglas put Huck's money in the bank, and Judge Thatcher did the same with Tom's. Each lad now had a dollar for every week-day in the year and half of the Sundays.

Huck went to live with the widow. Her servants kept him clean and neat. He slept every night in a bed. He had to eat with knife and fork; he had to use cup and plate; he had to learn to read; he had to go to church; he had to speak properly.

He stood it for three long weeks, and then one day he ran away. For two days the widow hunted for him everywhere. The people of the village looked high and low. They dragged the river for his body. Early the third morning Tom Sawyer went poking among some old empty barrels behind a shed, and in one of them he found the missing Huck. The lad had slept there, and was now lying in the sun, smoking his pipe. He was very dirty, and he was wearing his old rags again. Tom told him how much worry he had been, and told him to go home. Huck looked very unhappy at this. He said :

"Don't talk about it, Tom. I've tried it, and it doesn't work. It isn't for me—I'm not used to it. The widow is good to me, but I can't stand her ways. She makes me get up at the same time every morning; she makes me wash and comb my hair; she won't let me sleep in the wood-shed. I have to go to church and I can't catch a fly in there, and I have to wear shoes on Sunday."

"Well, everybody does that, Huck."

"Tom, it makes no difference. I can't stand it. It's awful to be tied up like that. I've got to ask to go fishing; I've got to ask to go swimming; I've got to ask to do everything. The widow wouldn't let me smoke, she wouldn't let me shout. And she prayed all the time! I never saw such a woman! I had to go, Tom, I just had to. Being rich isn't everything. It's just worry and worry, and work and work, and wishing you were dead all the time. Tom, I should never have got into all this trouble if it hadn't been for that money. You just take my share, and give me ten cents sometimes. And tell the widow I don't want to come back!"

"Oh, Huck, you know I can't do that. It isn't fair; and besides, if you try this thing a bit longer you'll begin to like it."

"Like it! Yes—the way I'd like a hot stove if I sat on it. No, Tom, I won't be rich, and I won't live in a house. I like the woods, and the river, and the empty barrels, and I'll stick to them, too. Hang it all! Just as we had got a cave and were all set to rob, this nonsense comes up and spoils it all!"

"Look here," said Tom, "being rich isn't going to stop me from being a robber."

"No? Do you mean that, Tom?"

"As sure as I'm sitting here. But, Huck, we can't let you join the gang if you don't look all right, you know."

"Can't let me join, Tom? Haven't you always been my friend? You wouldn't shut me out, would you? You wouldn't do that, now, would you, Tom?"

"Huck, I wouldn't want to, but what would people say? Why, they'd say 'Mph! Tom Sawyer's Gang! they're a pretty poor lot!' They'd mean you, Huck. You wouldn't like that, and I wouldn't."

Huck was silent for some time. At last he said:

"Well, I'll go back to the widow for a month and see if I can stand it, if you let me join the gang."

"All right, Huck, then I will. Come along, old chap, and I'll ask the widow to make things easier for you."

"Will you, Tom, now will you? That's good. When are you going to start the gang and turn robbers?"

"Oh, we'll start now. We'll get the boys together, and have the initiation to-night, maybe."

"Have what?"

"Have the initiation."

"What's that?"

"It's to say on oath that you'll stand by one another, and never tell the gang's secrets, even if you are chopped all to pieces. And you promise to kill anybody that hurts one of the gang."

"That's fine—that's really fine, Tom, I tell you."

"Well, I bet it is. And we have to do it at midnight in the most frightening place we can find. A haunted house is the best—but they are all torn up, now."

"Well, midnight's good, anyway, Tom."

"Yes, so it is. And you have to make your promise on a coffin, and sign your name with blood."

"Now that's something like! I'll stick to the widow till I die, Tom; and if I get to be a really good robber, and everybody talks about it, I reckon she'll be very pleased she took me in out of the wet."